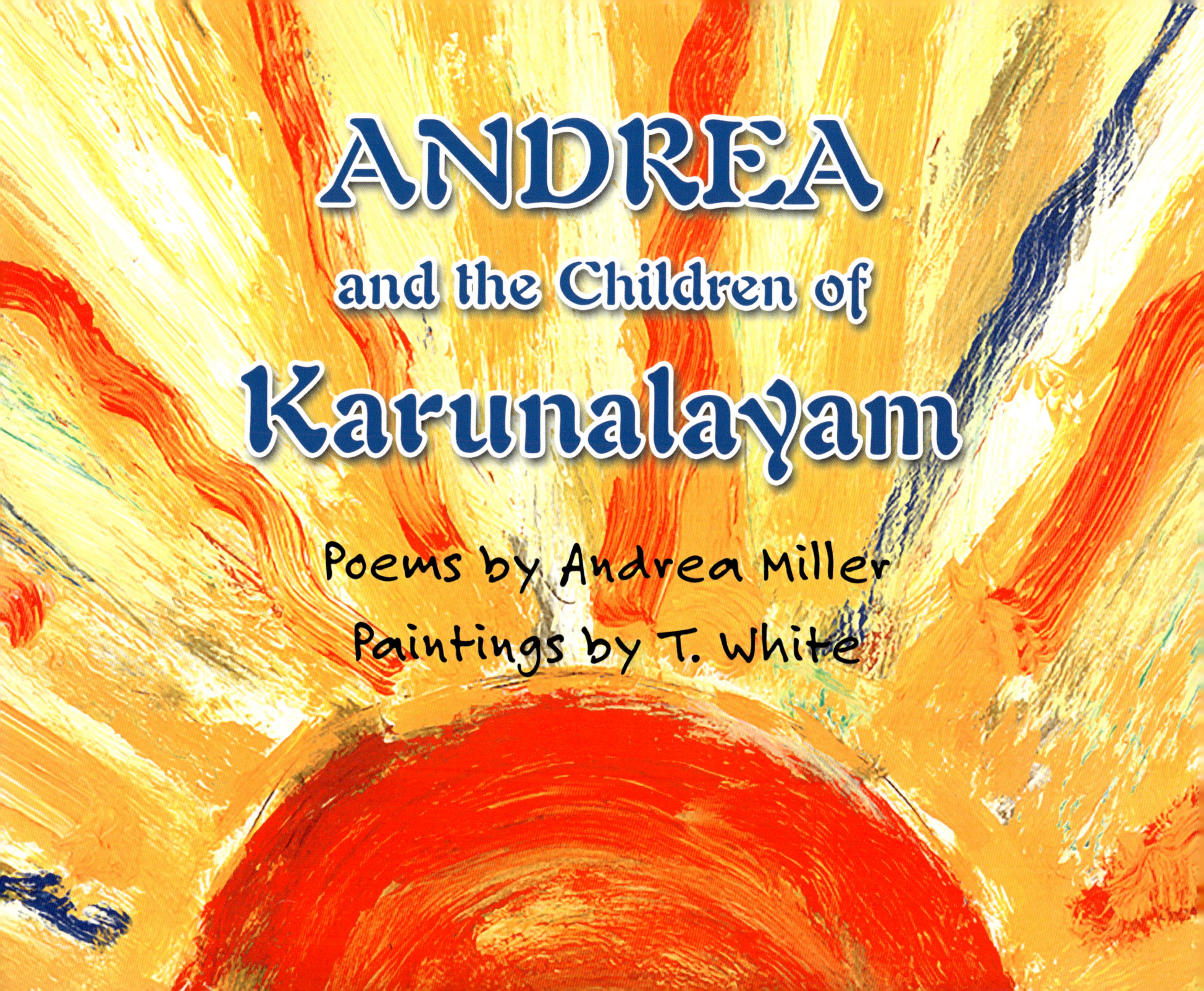

Deep in the heart of India are the orphan girls of Karunalayam. Sometimes life is hard, but through suffering comes hope for the children, and a little girl on the other side of the world.

Andrea's birth and first year of infancy were normal. But, as time went on, the monster made itself known.... Andrea had a malignant brain tumor. Because of the location, surgery could only partially remove the tumor. Doctors explained the grim prognosis to Andrea's parents. With chemotherapy and radiation, maybe she would have a 10% chance of living.... even then, it was unlikely she would ever learn to walk. But miracles do happen. Not only did Andrea survive, but she can walk and ride a bike. However, she still suffers; her eyes do not focus well together and grow bleary with use. She has a shunt in her skull. She suffers from headaches and minor strokes, and her hands shake with much use.

One day when Andrea was in school, her teacher's stories of poor orphaned girls in India moved Andrea to take action on behalf of others. A bluntly worded letter campaign, handwritten to friends and neighbors, raised enough money for the orphans to get school supplies and new outfits. Andrea's philosophical mentor, T. White, then suggested she paint a picture of "her girls" in India. After 15 weeks at the easel, the painting was completed. People from all over sent donations to this humble girl and received a print of her fine art work, and sometimes a poem from Andrea.

Andrea reads the Bible daily and makes sure her faith is something she expresses day-to-day, not relegated to an hour on Sundays. Her favorite story in the Bible is that of Moses. She appreciates that although Moses could have been a pharaoh, he instead followed the path of God. Andrea has a gentle soul and is convinced the reason God let her live was to help other people. Andrea stands out through her humility, passionate work and loving attitude. She truly believes there are blessings in everything, even when there has been heartache.

This little book contains the poems of a blessed and inspired girl with a fervent conviction to help those less fortunate than herself. All profits from the sale of this book go to benefit those in need.

Visitors

Why does one need a large house to share ideas?

The open air is large enough for the complete mass of the world

It is difficult to entertain many

So sit down and share your designs with a few

It is said that one expands one's knowledge simply by the art of listening

Why do we not have a quiet spell and listen to our hearts?

The children and the slaves seek a refuge

And He lets them in with open arms

Let us not overstay our welcome

But purely enjoy the company of our fellow man

Solitude

If we sit down for just one moment and listen to all the splendor of nature

We perhaps may learn something far beyond the books

By following our own schedule of self- realization

We learn to find ourselves in unexpected places

A man can make his own path in nature

Why should we want to follow the paths already made?

Nature is one's companion

We can be alone in nature and feel the greatest sentiment of friendship

Can we tell in this life what is truly lonely?

The spider works her web unaided and the beaver builds his dam unassisted

How lonely are these creatures of God?

For their companion is their Creator

Neighbors

The loon is so immensely graceful

It moves with the water as it continues on its path

The robin builds her nest for her young ones

She retrieves the food for their nourishment

The young ones are protected in their mother's care

Consider the mouse that scurries away when humans come close

We scare the poor creature back to its hole to stay there in endless captivity

The finch sings for our pleasure

It moves with the beat of life

The ants battle pending to the death

Are they not like our own flesh and blood?

Humans quarrel, but what is the reason for it?

We do not know, nor do we seem to grasp, the response

Is it true that the cause we fight for is just?

How can we know if our motives are not clear?

Humans are but a shadow of what various animals are akin to

Perhaps if we quarrel less, we will have more time for understanding

Don't Forget: God Loves You!

Do not try to forget the past

But remember God's promises for the future

Do not struggle to erase the sorrows from your heart

Think of the joys to come

Do not bundle fear and concern inside of you

Let your joy overflow like a river

Do not reward hate with revenge

Be kind to even the most hateful

Do not shun the unbeliever

Share God's work with all those who doubt

Do not seek justice when injustice is done to you

Love even your biggest enemy

Do not hate, but love

Do not despair, but have hope

Never forget that your Father in heaven loves you

He will make your sorrow into tears of joy

And your pain into wails of happiness

Alright

You hear the bird's call

You see the trees tall

Your hear the quiet river run

You listen to the children having fun

You look up to the moonlight

In the darkness of the night

You see the stars tiny light

And you know everything will be all right

Society

Young youth is zealous for life

For they do not know the sorrows of men

The age of men give the impression of discontentment towards life

They have not learned the happiness of young minds

Many men are not content with the life they lead

Perhaps that is because they lead no real life at all

They are walking down the path of a life that is not their own

Our lives are a pattern of repetition

We get up with the sun and go to bed with the moon

The circle seems to grow ever smaller

This grand experiment of life wastes away

How many of us have tried it?

The provisions of life are but very few

Merely food, water and shelter shall satisfy for a day on the earth

Whoever wants more than these shall always need more

Whoever is content with these, will need no more

Nature's Course

The world is going at a rapid pace

We might trip over our own feet if we do not slow down

The magnificence will not catch up to us!

We cannot even tell the pace of nature

How fast is it going in our mind's eye?

We cannot lose respect for nature

For who has thoroughly experienced it?

If we learn to take our medicine

Perchance we will find our diseases cured

Never Leave Me, Never Forsake Me

You never leave me, you're always there

You always understand, you always care

You never let me fall, you're the One that keeps me going

My heart is always loving, and my mind is always knowing

This journey may be hard, but you know best

And when I am tired, you let me rest

You help me up and then we go on

You never stop until my battle's won

You are the true victor, the one true King

My heart loves you more than any earthly thing

It's so breathtaking knowing how much

You want me to be able to touch

Your heart of gold, your hands of grace

I will come someday to your Holy Place

You want me to live, and not to die

So by your gift, I, too, may fly

Life

The luxuries in life are but materialistic distractions

One can live hopefully if simply they live uncommitted

Perhaps all we need is to live life

If an individual grasps the reality of the day

They will have a glimpse of eternity tomorrow

The day is when we are awake, the day is when we are alive

Why do we try to close our eyes during this segment of life?

Do we like to sleep and let the world overtake us?

We are missing something by not living life

Let us build our ship and sail in the direction of our own dreams

Where there is a hope for the day, there is a dream to believe in

Thinking of You

I was thinking of you the other day

And I couldn't help but cry

Knowing for me, you freely chose to die

Knowing how much you love me

I can hardly take it in

You took upon yourself, the cost of all my sin

Taking your hand, I'll rise with you

Leaving behind my sin and shame

I will praise your holy name

I was thinking of you the other day

How you guide me with a gentle hand

And keep my feet from the sinking sand

You are more precious to me than silver or gold

I'd give my life to be with you

You are the sun that shines through in all that I do

You are the true giver of true joy

The warmth of your love burns in my soul

You have a heart of true gold

I am thinking of you all the time

My heart inside me wants to sing

To only my Lord, my Father, my King

The Right Path

Behind their backs they speak lies about them

Who knows what their gossip contains?

They are so consumed by it; they do not know their own selves!

At night they cannot find the way to their shelter

The whisper of nature chills their souls

They have traveled the identical path several times

Yet their souls are lost upon it

Perhaps it is that they have lost faith in this road

Truly, until we have lost this world

We will not find ourselves

Why do we look when we know not where to?

They lock their homes at dusk

Is there truly anything more valuable than life?

He sails away to his ship in the forest

He is the captain of his own existence

If we all would simply find ourselves such as he has,

We could conceivably live this life!

Finished

Let us not follow the path of our friends

But let us step to the music we hear

We should learn the desires of our hearts

We need to build our own mast for our ship

We need to love the hand we are dealt

It is the only way to happiness

Seek the truth and you shall find it

The truth alone will set one free

Do not worry about reputation for the sake of truth

Build your castle where you please

Set the foundation on truth

Do not have any definition

Follow the beat of your heart

Rules are but a curse to this world

We follow what we cannot comprehend

Life seems to be the shortest it has ever been!

Andrea
and the Children of
Karunalayam

Poems by Andrea Miller

Paintings by T. White

copyright © 2005

All rights reserved. No part of this book may be reproduced or transmitted in any form or by any means, electronic or mechanical, including photocopying, recording, or by any information storage and retrieval system without permission in writing from the publisher. Published in the United States by T. White Art.

Manufactured in the United States

Library of Congress
Cataloging-in-publication data

ISBN NUMBER
0-9639670-4-5

First Edition

Production and Printing costs funded by Finishing Solutions, Inc.

Graphic Design by Fine Eye Imaging

Tax deductible donations can be mailed to:

**Andrea Miller Foundation
P.O. Box 163
Excelsior, MN 55331**

www.andreamillerfoundation.com